Joan Kufrin

write tight edit tough®

Your job depends on it.

table of contents

For **Wholesale orders,** please contact:
Ingram Group Inc.
www.ingramcontent.com
phone: 615.793.5000

For **Individual orders,** Write Tight, Edit Tough® is
available **on Amazon (U.S.)**
or as a Kindle book.

© 2013 Joan Kufrin | American Studio Press
ISBN-13: 978-1492357162
ISBN-10: 1492357162

https://www.writetight-edittough.com

Design: Bob Feie

preface

A few years ago, a professor challenged me to write a business writer's guide that was "short, simple and easy to understand." He didn't think it could be done; I knew otherwise.

Short, simple and easy to understand have been fixed stars for me during a long writing career. They also meshed with my other constant goal: to write copy that people want to read.

I took on his challenge. Write Tight, Edit Tough® is the result. (Acronym: WTET)

In it, I spell out the four essentials—yes, four are all you need—to write any business document, plus the two essentials you need to edit all copy.

To keep these essentials front of mind, I've linked them to commands familiar to every computer user. (You'll never think of Bold, Center, Enter, Shift, Select, Insert, Edit, Delete, Quit or Escape in the same way again.)

I've also consulted other business writers and added material they suggested, such as outlines and examples of typical business documents. In addition, I've included FAQs about grammar, usage and meaning of words.

You'll find that WriteTight, EditTough® is the one business writer's guide to focus only on the essentials of writing and editing that result in lean, muscular, powerful copy. The kind of copy people read.

I dedicate this guide to every business writer out there who must daily transform the complex, the minute, the mundane and yes, even the boring, into the compelling, using nothing more than words to make it soar.

Prepare for take-off.

Joan Kufrin
Chicago, Illinois
July 29, 2013

what business writers do and don't do

Welcome to WriteTight, EditTough,® the practical, no-sweat method for turning out lean, targeted, powerful copy on every project. Every time.

WriteTight, EditTough® will help you:

Understand what business writing is and is not;

Express complex ideas in clear, succinct copy using a minimum of words;

Write any business document with a subject, premise, body of content paragraphs and a conclusion;

Build and use a business vocabulary of verbs and nouns;

Write in the active voice;

Use these skills to edit your own copy and that of others.

Tools you'll need:

One portable combination dictionary/thesaurus. Computer programs do have a thesaurus feature but they are not comparable to a thesaurus in print. Two good ones:

Oxford Mini-Dictionary and Thesaurus with 65,000 synonyms

Barron's Pocket Dictionary & Thesaurus with 100,000 synonyms

How you'll learn

The following set of writing and editing concepts, named for familiar computer commands, will help keep you focused on ways to write tighter, leaner, and more powerful copy.

BOLD	**DELETE**
CENTER	**SHIFT**
ENTER	**QUIT**
SELECT	**ESCAPE**
INSERT	**EDIT**

Caveat: These commands don't automatically produce copy by pressing the appropriate key or command on a computer. They are simply easy-to-remember tools.

We'll go over these commands in more detail at the end of this chapter and as they apply to each concept.

Practice, practice, practice

Practical exercises reinforce the material of each chapter.

THE WRITER/READER CONTRACT

WriteTight, EditTough® is based on the assumption that there is an implied contract between a writer and a reader. This means we do not teach—and you are not here to learn—how to write words that fool people.

The writer/reader contract means we writers have a responsibility to write words that clearly denote our meaning. And, as readers who read what others write, we have a responsibility to not impose our own connotations on another writer's words.[1]

> **denotation:** a precise marking out; an exact defining.
> **connotation:** an implied or suggested meaning.

What is your role as a business writer?

You are the "voice" of a company (or organization) as it communicates precise information to those people who have a stake in that business, aka stakeholders.

External Stakeholders	Internal Stakeholders
Customers	Employees, including you
Shareholders	Management
Media	Boards of directors
Analysts	Unions
Government agencies	Retirees

THINK ABOUT: Choose one internal and one external group. How would your written communications to them be different? The same?

Why are business writers powerful...and potentially harmful?

Whatever you write affects the very groups who determine the ultimate success or failure of the company that employs you.

What functions do business writers serve?

Report and deliver news, good or bad
Disseminate information
Instruct
Persuade
Clarify complex issues
Document/track reality
Influence opinion

What do business writers not do?

Create art
Move people emotionally
Write for posterity

What are the results of imprecise, false or inconclusive business writing?

Delivers untruths, deliberate or not
Misinforms
Lacks instruction
Does not persuade...or communicate
Fails to simplify the complex
Does not document or track reality
Reinforces the status quo

In short, imprecise, wrong or inconclusive writing causes harm, costs time and money, damages image, affects sales and can contribute to a company's demise.

Key takeaway: As deliverers of precise information, business writers who are not precise, concise and targeted, fail the very companies that employ them.

What kind of writing is done for internal audiences?

Financial reports
Organizational strategies
Marketing plans
Case studies
Feasibility studies
Email
Social media

For external audiences?

Annual reports
Press eleases
Speeches
SEC filings
B2B
Email
Social media

What questions should you ask—and answer—before you write a single word of a business piece?

Who is the audience for your piece?
What are you writing about?
Why are you writing it?
When will it be read?
Where will it be read?
How will it be written?

We'll go into these questions in depth when we explore the common structure of every piece of business writing.

Key takeaway: Business writers determine who their audience/reader is before they write a single word, and then keep the writer/reader contract front of mind as they write.

What kind of writing turns readers off?

Huge blocks of copy, with no paragraph relief in sight;
Boring, repetitive, obscure writing;
Busy, distracting headlines and subheads; nothing and everything stands out;
Poor grammar and poor spelling.

What kind turns readers on?

> Sharp, compelling headlines;
> Brief, potent message(s) stated up front;
> Brief paragraphs (in longer pieces);
> Correct grammar and correct spelling.

The WriteTight, EditTough® COMPUTER COMMANDS

Again. These commands don't automatically produce copy by pressing the appropriate key on a computer. They are simply easy-to-remember tools to help you focus on ways to write tighter and more direct copy. We'll cover each of these commands in upcoming chapters.

BOLD verbs ignite readers' imaginations and **BOLD** nouns color your writing and reduce the need for modifiers.

CENTER the key idea of the piece in your mind.

ENTER it quickly in the title, subtitle, or lead paragraph because your first thought is often the freshest and the best.

SELECT active (transitive) verbs instead of "to be" verbs.

> **transitive verb:** conveys action from the subject to the object.
> **intransitive verb:** confines action to the subject.

INSERT the active voice for the passive voice wherever you find it.

DELETE qualifiers: the dull, the weak, the diminishing words. Eliminate the extraneous. Anything that does not support the key idea should go.

SHIFT not your point of view.

QUIT on a thoughtful note.

ESCAPE the mundane.

EDIT constantly, up through the final draft.

PRACTICE

Find two pieces of writing from current newspapers or magazines, print or digital, that include:

An example of writing that turns you off. You don't read it or you skim it and toss. Understand why.

Writing that turns you on. It caught your eye and you didn't put it down until you'd read all of it. Understand why.

Key takeaway: Understanding what makes you read one piece of writing and what makes you avoid another is the beginning of change.

List 15 verbs that are synonyms of the following verb "to make" or "bring into being." (These will begin your life list of power verbs and nouns.)

> **verb:** the part of speech that expresses action or being.
> **synonym:** a word that means the same, or nearly the same as another word.

the power verb

Power turns your computer on. Power words turn your reader on. The power words of the English language are **verbs** and **nouns.**

Of the two, the **verb** is the most essential word of a sentence. Why? A verb tells the reader what the subject is doing or what state of being the subject is in. The **verb** is the engine that propels your sentence. Without a verb, the sentence goes nowhere.

Kinds of Verbs

Action verbs are those that depict action, like "leap, dive, embrace, sing, eat." (Other examples?)

State of being verbs are forms of the words "to be." "Am, are, was, were, will be, has been," etc. To see all forms of the "to be" verb, go to FAQs, p. 57.

Of the two, action verbs **prove** the most powerful. Why? They **ignite** imagined movement in your reader's brain. **See** the *Declaration of Independence* for superb use of action verbs. **Selecting** action verbs instead of "to be" verbs will **build** muscle in your writing.

In the sentence "I was here," ("was" is a form of the state of being verb "to be"), how can you make this a much stronger sentence, one that engages the reader's imagination, one that will **ESCAPE** the mundane?

Substitute an action verb for the "to be" verb "was." Possibilities: I **jogged** here. I **crawled** here. I **danced** here. I **hopped** here. I **pirouetted** here. I **dragged** myself here. See the verbal image in your brain?

In these three lists of similar action verbs, which elicit the most powerful image in your mind's eye?

leap	jump	spring
tackle	embrace	enfold
pinch	crush	mash
march	stroll	amble

Key takeaway: Action verbs ignite the imagination in your reader's mind.

However. When there is no other verb to use than a "to be" verb, use it without hesitation. You'll know when.

WTET introduces the three **COMPUTER COMMANDS** that most affect the verb:

> **BOLD** reminds us to use power verbs, aka action verbs.
>
> To **ESCAPE** the mundane reminds us why we use power verbs.
>
> **SELECT** action verbs instead of "to be" verbs for strong, concise

writing.

> **10-MINUTE POP EXERCISE**
> Write a 50-word description of yourself without using any form of the verb "to be."

REVIEW the **passive voice** versus the **active voice.**

> In the **passive voice,** the subject of the verb **receives** the action.
>
> > **ex:** Record profits **were produced** by the direct marketing team. The quarterly report **was released** by the vice president. You **are loved** by me.
>
> In the **active voice,** the subject of the verb **does** the action and the object of the verb **receives** the action.
>
> > **ex:** Our direct marketing team **produced** record profits. The vice president **released** the quarterly figures. I **love** you.
>
> Why use the **active voice** instead of the **passive voice?**
>
> > Simpler
> > Shorter
> > More direct
> > More forceful
> > Faster
> > Stronger
>
> **Caveat:** There is a role for the **passive voice.** It is best used for **emphasis.** To emphasize a point, position your main point at the beginning of a sentence and use the passive voice. **Example:** Record profits **were due** to increased participation by every single employee.

Clarity. If it's not clear who or what is doing the action, use the passive voice to help the reader.

> **ex:**   Stores **were invaded** by early morning shoppers.

Or, if the subject of the verb is not as important as the object.

> **ex:**   The CEO **was subjected** to shareholders' anger.

WTET introduces the **COMPUTER COMMAND:**

> **INSERT** the active voice for the passive voice wherever you find it, unless the passive voice is needed for any of the three preceding reasons.

REVIEW the **adverb,** a modifier.

> An **adverb** is the part of speech that modifies a verb, an adjective, or another adverb, and usually answers the questions **how, where, why, when** and **to what degree.**

> Most adverbs are formed by adding "ly" to an adjective. Thus the adjective beautiful becomes the adverb beautifully.[2]

> **Q.**   Which of the following are more precise and concise?

> > **ex:**   The man walked **slowly** and **aimlessly** along the beach.

> > or: The man **ambled** along the beach.
> > The man **strolled** the beach.
> > The man **shuffled** along the beach.
> > He **trudged** along the beach.

> > **ex:**   The man walked **purposefully** and **quickly** down the road.

> > or: The man **strode** down the road.
> > The man **marched** down the road.
> > The man **patrolled** the road.

To WTET writers, adverbs have little use other than to bloat sentences. Their main job is to modify other modifiers. Most writers use them to prop up weak verbs, which they wouldn't need to do if they had used the strongest verbs they could find in the first place.

Key takeaway: Let muscular verbs do the heavy work to spare your readers from plowing through thickets of modifiers, i.e. adverbs.

WTET Introduces the **COMPUTER COMMAND:**

DELETE qualifiers, modifiers (such as adverbs) and extraneous words whenever possible.

Review **COMPUTER COMMANDS thus far:**

BOLD verbs for concise and strong writing.

ESCAPE the mundane by using **BOLD** verbs.

SELECT action verbs instead of "to be" verbs

INSERT active voice for the passive voice wherever you find it.

PRACTICE

List 10 verbs that are synonyms for the verb "to encourage."

List 15 nouns that are synonyms for the noun "employee."

Draft a letter to a prospective employee, someone you really want to hire. Your company has recently downsized and your prospect knows it. Your company has also recently been involved in a product safety recall. Your letter will try to persuade this person to work for you.

Read your all-action-verb 50-word self profile aloud.

Review your list of 15 verbs that are synonyms of "make."
(Here are some, scrambled.)

dropceau	mofr
erteca	trucncost
scompeo	ifonash
bactefia	remaf
edvesi	negsid
tanfurmaceu	shisbeatl
aveew	gorfe
goritaien	

the precise noun

Power turns your computer on. Power words turn your reader on. Meet the second most powerful word in the English language: the **noun.**

A noun tells the who, the what and where of the sentence. Specifically, **nouns** name **persons** (teachers), **places** (New York), **things** (trees), **states** (health) or **qualities** (intelligence). Nouns can act as subjects or objects of a verb's action or as objects of prepositions.

If verbs are the engines that propel a sentence, nouns are its first-class passengers.

REVIEW kinds of **nouns**

> **Proper** nouns name individual persons (Jane) and places (Spain) and are always capitalized.

> **Common** nouns name the class of items, not the particular item (flowers) (schools) and are not capitalized, except at the beginning of sentences.

> **ex:**   Flowers cheer a room. These flowers are for you.

> **THINK ABOUT**—Why are nouns the second most powerful part of speech?

> They evoke the same (or similar) image in your reader's mind. The more precise the noun you use, the more precise the connection with your reader.

> **Q.**   Which noun is more specific and thus has a more precise connection to your reader's mind?

(a) the employees	(b) the staff	(c) the designers
(a) my secretary	(b) my assistant	(c) my right-hand
(a) report	(b) plan	(c) strategy

> **Q.**   Which noun is more powerful and thus makes a faster connection with your reader's mind?

> (a) deadline; priority; front burner;
> (b) problem; dilemma; puzzle; predicament; jam; crisis;

PRACTICE

> Using your thesaurus, find ten synonyms for the following nouns and identify the most and least powerful. Keep the strongest ones for your life list.

> skill
> load
> list

For your next writing assignment at work, replace nouns that are repetitive, familiar and/or boring with precise, muscular and colorful nouns.

REVIEW the **adjective,** a modifier

An **adjective** is a part of speech that describes or modifies a noun (or pronoun, p. 59) and usually answers the questions **which, what kind of, how many, how much.**

ex: windy, tiny, spectacular, handsome

An adjective cannot stand alone. It needs a noun to make sense. But a noun can stand alone. It doesn't need an adjective. Try not to use adjectives.

The more powerful the noun you use (one without an adjective to modify it), the faster your connection with the reader. Here are some bold nouns that grab a reader's attention and incite instant connections—without modifiers.

Tsunami.   Rattlesnake.   Cancer.   Profits.   Bankruptcy.

WTET: The three **COMPUTER COMMANDS** that affect the noun:

BOLD is the computer command that reminds you of their power.

BOLD nouns are memorable, grab the reader's attention and make instant connections. Most important, they

ESCAPE the mundane.

DELETE their qualifiers, the adjectives; also, any dull, weak and extraneous words.

Key takeaway:

"Write with nouns and verbs, not with adjectives or adverbs. The adjective hasn't been built that can pull a weak or inaccurate noun out of a tight place."[3]

A NOTE ON BREVITY IN WRITING

If you use the following quotation in any way, please credit: Arthur Kudner, founder/partner of Erwin, Wasey & Co., and Arthur Kudner, Inc., advertising agencies.

Big, Long Words...

Big long words name little things.
All big things have little names,
Such as life and death, peace and war
Or dawn, day, night, hope, love, home.
Learn to use little words in a big way.
It is hard to do.
But they say what you mean.
When you don't know what you mean—
Use big words.
That often fools little people.

Art Kudner

A NOTE ON REALISM IN WRITING

And, if you use the following quotation, please credit the visionary who founded his advertising agency, The Leo Burnett Company, during the middle of the Great Depression:

"If you are writing about baloney, don't try to make it Cornish hen, because that is the worst kind of baloney there is. Just make it darned good baloney."

Leo Burnett

REVIEW your list of power verbs that mean "to encourage."

plhe	weepmowr
srinipe	genud
efir pu	tormepo
grivonitea	orfset
guer	tissas
prosput	

Also the 15 nouns for "employee."

tissantsa	tspsielcai
gramane	kwor efcro
texucevi	rceokwro
rovnnite	eotfafmiec
lennesorp	rfeeklrlooww
fatsf	trexep
geulleaoc	traminaditors
	repe

Key takeaway: WriteTight,EditTough® suggests **that you refrain from referring to employees as "new hires" or "head counts," or that a company has "taken a haircut" when you mean it has fired or let go a number of workers.**

PRACTICE

Add 10 verbs meaning to fire an employee to your list of power verbs. (Here are some, scrambled.)

tle og	trieer
ganeirss	simidss
toorpinesi	qosueoz tue
ecelotre	sleares
gadresich	ucert foo

Collect seven headlines that grabbed you and analyze why they did.

the same structure
for all business writing

Now, we come to the reason we're all here: writing a business document.

All business writing, except the blog, shares the same structure that can be adapted to every document. These are its components.

SUBJECT	Presents the key idea of the piece (or study, plan, strategy, press release) also known as the title.	**What**
PREMISE	Briefly states your purpose in writing the piece. It can be as short as a subtitle for the piece or its lead paragraph.	**Why**
BODY	Targeted to your readers, this collection of separate paragraphs informs, persuades, argues or documents the subject for the reader's consideration.	**Who**
CONCLUSION	Summarizes the preceding material into a course of action or a resolution.	**How**

The above components are listed in their usual order. That sounds easy. But when you're looking at a blank computer screen or a blank piece of paper as a hundred thoughts bombard your brain, how do you sort through all the data you've gathered and bring coherence to your piece? Let's begin with the first item.

Subject:

To pin it down, ask yourself the question: **what** is the piece about? To help you do this, **WTET** introduces three of the most useful computer commands:

    CENTER the key idea in your mind (Zen-like);

    ENTER it quickly on paper or computer. This will be your working title. Do it quickly. Your first thought is often your best and your freshest.

    SHIFT not your subject, once you've found it.

    EX: Should ABCORP Build New Headquarters?

The subject will anchor your entire piece but its title must be compelling. You want to grab the attention of your readers, not cause their eyeballs to glaze over. So make the title short. Try for six words or less, whether it's a financial report, feasibility study, marketing plan, press release or email. The title will lead readers to the premise of your piece.

Premise

The premise addresses the question of **why** you are writing the piece. Answer that question and quickly **ENTER** it on a computer or paper as a subtitle or a short lead paragraph to tell the reader what's coming next. Again, speed is vital because your first thoughts often turn out to be the freshest and the best. (You can always change the wording later.)

> ex: **A new look at a 75-year-old structure**

Body

Before you write a word, ask yourself who is the target audience? Your staff? Your boss? The CEO? Shareholders? The body of your piece is made up of a group of related paragraphs that will then inform, solve, persuade, argue and/ or document the subject for your target audience.

> **Paragraphs** are the units in which you will develop the logic of your written piece. As you know, a paragraph is made up of a group of *sentences* that deals with one particular idea, or *topic*.

> Each paragraph is indented or set apart with a blank line like this, to alert the reader that a change in the topic or idea is coming. In a formal paper, each paragraph is called a topic paragraph.

> **Sentences,** which develop the topic of each paragraph, are the basic connectors between you, the writer, and your reader. Your sentences reveal to your reader whether you are thoughtful, a phony or a fool. Thus, the sentences that make up a paragraph are your golden opportunity to write tight, strong copy that best develops and furthers your subject. Like bricks, sentences build your case, one by one.

> Eliminate any sentence that does not support the topic of the paragraph. Prune **(EDIT)** constantly. Above all, as you write, **SHIFT not** your point of view.

For years we've followed the rule that every sentence should be complete, that is, contain at least one main clause made up of an independent subject and verb.[4]

ex: "Being of sound mind" is not a complete sentence because there is no independent subject or verb. Neither is this a complete sentence: "A natural inquiry, given Canada's endless to-do list of breathtaking destinations, thriving cities and unique cultural experiences." (From *This is Canada, Summer 2011*).

Caveat: Know that the complete sentence rule is being ignored by *The New York Times. Newsweek. Time.* To name a few. Sometimes, incomplete sentences do yeoman work. Like stopping readers in their tracks. Grabbing attention. Focusing on an idea. Like this. If you want to use an incomplete sentence, do so without angst.

Conclusion

Relate your conclusion directly to the subject of the piece. State it concisely. If there are several conclusions, list them from the most important, all drawn from the body of logical paragraphs.

Recommendations:

Often, writers are asked for their recommendations regarding the subject of the piece. Give them here.

As you write, remember the **COMPUTER COMMANDS:**

SELECT action verbs over "to be" verbs whenever possible.

INSERT the active voice for the passive voice;
BOLD VERBS AND NOUNS;
To these, **WTET** introduces a new **COMPUTER COMMAND:**
QUIT on a note that will keep your readers thinking about your piece.

ex: What do you think? Should a 75-year old building continue to house the 21st century, tech pioneer ABCORP?

REVIEW

The four WriteTight® essentials;

1. Write with power verbs and precise nouns, to avoid using adverbs and adjectives.

2. Write in the active voice instead of the passive voice.

3. Use action verbs instead of forms of the "to be" verb.

4. Use the same basic structure for all business documents, which answers the questions:

What am I writing about?	Subject
Why am I writing it?	Premise
Who am I explaining it to?	Body
How is it resolved?	Conclusion(s)
When, where	(If pertinent)

PRACTICE

Study the seven compelling headlines you've gathered and decide why they're compelling.

Write short headlines for the following hypothetical stories:

An amputee lands the lead in a local ballet production;

True green (organic) vegetables are being grown locally and delivered to city farmers' markets weekly;

A company begins hiring again, but only temporary employees.

Write a confidential memo from a vp/development to the CEO urging the company to consider moving or building new quarters using this background:

ABCORP, a company with $100 million in sales, makes space-age faucets for homes and businesses and has done so for 75 years, in the same vintage building.

Use the structure in this lesson, the active voice, precise nouns, action verbs and a minimum of modifiers.

why to write without modals

The following nine unique words are called modals.[5]

can	may
could	might
should	must
would	will
shall	

They are also called auxiliary verbs, because they are always used in combination with other verbs. Modals have the extraordinary ability to alter the meaning of any verb they're attached to in subtle and powerful ways.

Simply by the context in which it is used, a modal, like a chameleon, changes the definition of a verb to mean an ability, a necessity, uncertainty, emphasis, possibility, a habit, a prediction, a suggestion, the future, a conditional state, negation, permission or a question.[6]

ACTIVITY—Working with modals

If we attach one of the above modals to a verb, we instantly change its meaning. Consider the verb "walk." See what happens when we use any of the modals above.

"I **can** walk," means I have the ability to walk. Or, I have permission to walk. Or, I can possibly walk, not drive. Inverted, "Can I walk?" becomes a question for all these possibilities.

"I **could** walk," means I have the ability to walk or I'm given permission to walk. It's also a possibility for me to get where I want to go. Inverted, "Could I walk?" becomes a question or also a possibility.

"I **should** walk," is advice from my doctor. Or, it's a suggestion from a friend who knows the area. Or it's a prediction based on good weather, perhaps. "Should I walk?" also expresses uncertainty.

"I **would** walk," because it's an old habit of mine since childhood or it's conditional if you would walk, too. It's my preference, rather than ride a bike, or, if I were given permission to. Inverted, "Would I walk there?" asks a question about the distance I need to travel. "You would walk," is a suggestion made to you. "Would you walk with me?" becomes an invitation.

"I **shall** walk" is an emphatic decision. Or it's something I'll do in the future. Or it's a habit of mine, like dieting. Inverted, "Shall I walk?" is a question. "Shall we walk?" is an invitation.

"I **may** walk" is a probability. "May I walk?" asks permission.

"I **might** walk" is both a possibility or a probability. "You might walk," is a suggestion, and also a possibility or a probability.

"I **must** walk" is a necessity flowing from the statement "My car has broken down." Or, it is a necessity because I never have money for cabs or buses, nor do I have a bicycle. "I must walk three miles a day" because it's a habit of mine. "I must not walk" because I am prohibited from doing so by the traffic light.

"I **will** walk" is a plan for the future. "I will walk with you" is an emphatic suggestion. "Will you walk?" is a question to ask a friend who is coming to visit you. "Will you walk home, please, and forget about a movie tonight?" is a suggestion to your tipsy friend.

Now that you know what modals are capable of, if you find yourself writing one of them in a press release or obituary, or in most business documents,

WTET introduces the following **COMPUTER COMMAND:**

> **DELETE** it.

> Why? Because modals, while versatile, are also ambiguous, instill possibility and probability, vacillate between suggestion and indecision, imply choice, offer suggestions, request permission and ultimately do not contribute to clear, concise writing.

> **Key takeaway: Use the COMPUTER COMMAND to DELETE all qualifiers; all dull, weak, and diminishing words; and most modals.**

> **Caveat:** every rule exists to be broken. There are times when a modal is necessary and nothing else will do.

> **ex:**   I must stop that fight!

If you want to hear modals used constantly, watch—and listen to—cable television. Its news writers are enamored of, and use modals to the near extinction of fact and observation.

PRACTICE

Write a one-page press release or a sales report in which one or more modals are necessary to the information.

Tally the number of modals used in a half-hour cable TV news program, vs. a network TV news program or a half-hour of PBS news.

Add 15 synonyms for the verb "consider" to your life-list of verbs.

mtceaploent	rodpen	tfencle ro
gihwe	rolmeluv	teadebrlei
seum	nmodeett ai	cusssdi
axnemie	netrmuia	getctaio
dtusy	drager	duejg

the business email

Business email delivers information anywhere on the planet, within seconds, to any stakeholder in a company's business, via electronic messages sent and received over the Internet.

Email is fast, easy[7] and has revolutionized the way business communicates. However, if you think email is the best mail system ever devised, consider this:

Email isn't that fast.

To send, maybe, but we *receive* so much we spend 2.6 hours of our business day--or 120 pages--reading, forwarding or otherwise "handling" our email.[8]

Email is permanent.

Fact: When investigating white collar crime, the F.B.I., the U.S. attorney, individual states' attorneys and/or police departments often utilize subpoenas and court orders to seize a suspect's computer, go into its hard drive and print out every email that person has ever written, even though the mail has been deleted from visible files.[9]

Key takeaway: "Deleted"emails exist forever on your hard drive.

Email is out of your control as soon as you send it.

Your recipient can forward it to any computer in the world with a keystroke.

Key takeaway: Consider every email a potentially public document.

Company emails are not yours, even if you send or receive them.

Most companies require employees to sign an agreement to honor its email policy. Even if yours has no written email policy, know this:

Key takeaway: Your company owns every email you write and send on company equipment or that is stored on company equipment. This includes any private emails you receive or send during the business day.

Key takeaway: Internet browsing is great for research but it opens possible breaches of confidentiality of your company's information and/or contamination of the company's system through viruses or spyware.[10] Access the Internet on company time only for company business.

Email has unintended consequences.

No matter what the subject line is, the email you write reveals personal information about you that transcends words. Namely:

> your character;
> your intelligence;
> your ability to think and reason;
> what you like and dislike;
> what you think is funny;
> your work habits, which reflect your personal habits;
> the degree of respect you have for others and yourself;
> your grammar and writing skills;

Key takeaway:
Turn on your third "reader's eye" to monitor, edit, or challenge every sentence and thought in your email before you hit the "send" button. If you don't, your recipient will find every mistake you've overlooked, often with glee.

Email wastes (big) time. Chief complaints:

> Too wordy
> Doesn't get to the point
> Sloppy spelling, grammar, and syntax
> Wrong tone
> Wrong subject choice

The WriteTight, EditTough® email goal: Shorten it and they will read it.

To turn out brief, targeted, error-free email that says what you mean and means what you say, ask six questions before you write one word.

Why am I writing this?

> - All emails either ask for something or tell something.[11]
> - Reality check: would a phone call/voice mail have more impact than this email? If so, make the phone call instead.

What am I writing about?

> - What is my main point?
>
> **Hint:** Write a subject line with an action verb and a precise noun that become the entire email. The best part? You know it will be read.

ex. re: Help the Help Desk. Friday a.m. 9-1. RSVP now.
re: Need your ideas at 3, Thurs., my office. Confirm.
re: Brainstorm Ajax' PR needs today at 2. Room 210.

Who will receive this email? That person is your **only** focus.

- If there are multiple recipients who have the same background and knowledge of the subject, send everyone the same email.
- If not, tailor the message for each reader and send separate emails.

How should you write it?

Assume your recipient has no time to read anything so position your key points front and center. Use bullet points for ease of reading only if you're sure bullet points translate to others' computers. Otherwise an ordinary list will do. One key point per line.

Ask for what you need in as few words as possible.

ex:

■ **Brief subject**	RE: Need EVP announcements for a.m. release tomorrow
■ **Friendly**	Hi, _____ (always include name) I know you've been going at full speed, but
■ **Accurate**	we need your turnaround skills on a promotions
■ **Clear**	announcement for three senior vps to executive vps,
■ **When**	by 4:00 p.m. today for release tomorrow.
■ **Next step**	Please call HR for details.
■ **Thanks**	Thanks for your consistent and able execution of deadline tasks.
■ **Tone**	Try for light-hearted and friendly, minus cute. Using the first and second person (I, we, you) will achieve this.
■ **Check**	Grammar and spelling.
■ **Double check**	Spelling of names.

Where is your email going?

For **international email** remove all jargon, idioms and figures of speech your non-U.S. recipients might misinterpret or may not understand.[12] They will welcome formality, respect and accuracy.

When do you send this email?

Always, when you ask or tell something that needs a rapid response.

Never, if it conveys or contains:

Anger
Confidential information
Complaints
Disagreements
Emoticons
Gossip
Gripes
Jokes/humor
Personnel issues
Sarcasm
Sexual material
Ultimatums
ALL CAPS (equals yelling)

Key takeaway: Before you send any email, ask yourself "Would I want to receive it?" If the answer is "no," don't send it.

WriteTight, EditTough® sample email format

To: Steer-O Account Team: Megan Stuart, Carla Leaf, Mac Singer, Tim Shahoda

From: Jean Green—CEO

RE: Steer-O Rewards Great Work

Steer-O Advertising Director, I. Arbro, has announced that our marketing program for Steer-O propelled sales 30 percent over last year. As a result, we will now:

> —Adapt the U.S. Steer-O marketing plan for Brazil's market;

> —Handle roll-out of the company's latest Product X (still under wraps);

> —Become lead agency for Product X through traditional and social media in the U.S.

Congratulations and thank you all for your dedication, drive and professionalism which led to landing this new business. Tomorrow we'll begin our new challenge with enthusiasm and vigor.

Jean Green (use full name)

(With in-company email, use your title only if it's a large organization.)

With outside mail, sign your email with full signature:

name
title
company
address
Phone:
Fax:
Mobile:
Email:
Website URL

Attachments

- In your email, alert recipient that a document is attached and what kind of attachment it is.
- Make sure it *is* attached before you send it.
- Best kind: PDF attachments that preserve formatting.
- Rich Text is universal and lets you send an attachment to anyone and the text will be preserved, though the formatting will likely not be.

> **Avoid computer-generated formatting** that might not show up on another computer: bold face, italics, bullets, lines, boxes, colors.

CC's and BCC's

The **CC** abbreviation tells the recipient a (carbon) copy of the letter has been sent to someone else who is also reading it.

BCC stands for blind carbon copy and it notifies only the recipient of the copy who receives it, not the person to whom you send the original email. Not recommended by WriteTight, EditTough® in the interest of harmonious, transparent business relationships.

Draft important messages offline

To keep from sending an important message before it's ready, draft it offline, then copy and paste it into the email. Only then add the email address.

Forwarding email

When you consider forwarding (inflicting) email on someone else, ask yourself:
> Do they need it?
> Do they want it?
> Do they care?

If the answer is "no" to any of the above, don't.

> **Key takeaway: Forward only the vital or the spellbinding.**

Long emails

Complicated, complex, long emails are better as a hard-copy letter or memo. However, if you must use email:

Present key ideas in an executive summary to begin.

Develop each idea in one paragraph.

Summarize that long email by echoing the key points that you used in the executive summary, but use different wording.

End with your own conclusion, recommendation, judgment or suggested course of action, if asked to do so.

Key takeaway: Long emails turn off readers. Forwarded material that doesn't concern the reader and attachments with un-paragraphed copy are also major turn-offs.

Key takeaway: If it doesn't have to go in, leave it out. Delete any word, thought or information that does not directly relate to the subject.

Spam fodder: The following words in the subject line ensure instant relegation to the SPAM folder:

> FYEO (for your eyes only)
> PROFIT
> LOOK AT THIS OFFER
> $$
> YOU'VE WON!

Email check list before you hit SEND:

- Subject line grabs attention and contains a strong verb and noun.
- Spelling is correct. Spell check is not always accurate because it can't tell the difference between you, yours, you're and your; to, two and too, singular and plural forms of a noun, etc.
- Double check the spelling of names of people receiving the email.
- Grammar is perfect. Tenses match. Nouns and verbs agree in number.
- Every fact is accurate and can be attributed.
- Attachments are indeed attached.
- Your signature and phone number close the email.
- You cannot proof an email too many times.

PRACTICE

Write two emails as if you have only 15 minutes each to get your message out on these subjects:

> You just learned the client has asked to attend the agency's strategy meeting this afternoon on its new "X" product. Alert the team.

> Your child is sent home ill from school. Ask a colleague or boss to take your place interviewing a prospective employee who is in town briefly to interview with you. Attach the prospective employee's resumé and the questions you were planning to ask her.

Review the last 10 emails you've received. Did they grab your attention, hold it, and goad you into action? Ask yourself if they did or didn't and why or why not.

Keep track, for one week, of the time you spend on email. Then vow to change how and what you send or forward as email.

edit tough® for clarity and vigor

Editing is the most enjoyable aspect of creating clear, vigorous copy.

Your mission as editor? To transform flawed, wordy, imprecise and/or difficult to understand documents, written by you or someone else, into lean, muscular, vibrant copy that a reader cannot ignore.

Here are the two EditTough® essentials for editing, whether you work on hard copy or do online editing.

1. Read/Think. (Hard)

a.   Read the material thoroughly, as often as necessary to understand it. Is the key idea at the **CENTER** of the piece? Check that the components of basic structure are in place: subject, premise, body, conclusion. Make sure the transitions between them are logical and clear. And check that the point of view did not **SHIFT** from beginning to end.

b.   Paraphrase the key thought/idea in each paragraph. Rewrite to simplify, if necessary. Follow this timeless advice:

"When you become hopelessly mired in a sentence, it is best to start fresh; do not try to fight your way through against the terrible odds of syntax. Usually what is wrong is that the construction has become too involved at some point; the sentence needs to be broken apart and replaced by two or more shorter sentences."[13]

c.   Does each paragraph build logically upon the preceding paragraph?

d.   Look up every word you don't know or think readers won't. Then, replace it with a simpler, more recognizable word **except** when using specialized i.e., scientific or technological vocabulary. (Include the layman's term if it will help readers.)

e.   Mark the subject and verb in each sentence. You'll need them for the next part of the editing process.

f.   Does the piece **QUIT** on a positive, thought-provoking note?

2. Pruning. (Fun) Remember **COMPUTER COMMANDS** for editing:

a.   **SELECT** any action verb instead of a "to be" verb, if possible.

ex: from: She has always been an excellent employee.

to: Daily, she delivers five-star work.

from: He is an opportunist.
to: He seizes every opportunity.

b.   **INSERT** any form of the passive voice with the active voice.

      ex: from: An increase of five percent productivity was accomplished.

             to: The team increased productivity by five per cent.

             from: The plan was approved unanimously.

             to: Management unanimously approved the plan.

c.   **DELETE** all adjectives and adverbs unless they are key descriptors: numbers, colors, dimensions, etc.

      DELETE qualifiers: just, a little; somewhat; I think; perhaps; maybe; in the first place; on the one hand; the fact of the matter is, etc.[14]

      DELETE the dull, the weak, the diminishing words, the extraneous. Anything that does not support the key idea should go.

d.   **BOLD** verbs and **BOLD** nouns **ESCAPE** the mundane.

Key takeaways:

SELECT action verbs instead of **"to be" verbs,** whenever possible.
INSERT the active voice for the passive voice wherever possible.
DELETE the redundant, the pedantic, the weak, the pompous, the dull, the qualifiers and whatever does not support the key idea.

PRACTICE

Read the following Example A. Using the numbered lines as reference, jot down the questions that need to be answered in order to edit the piece. Using the editing process, edit Example A and prepare a final edited copy. Compare yours with the WTET edited piece.

If you have time, **edit** Example B. Otherwise, read the WTET edit for Example B and compare with the unedited version.

Find a newspaper and make sure it contains obituaries.
Read them. Which make you wish you had known the deceased?
Understand why.

Add 20 synonyms for the noun "asset" to your life list.

tbeifne	evuitr	lcaaipt	ymeon
eadgavtan	phle	ercersuo	sganvi
sbglneis	dai	sreevser	hwtela
obon	tsrupop	sfdnu	sseeictuir
ngrehtts	ogod	shgonlid	smnae

Example A. (unedited)

Sub for a Day, Teacher Pension for Life

1 Two lobbyists with no prior teaching experience <u>were allowed</u> to count

2 their two years as union employees toward a state teacher pension once they

3 served a single day of subbing in 2007, a Tribune/WGN-TV investigation <u>has</u>

4 <u>found.</u>

5 Steven Preckwinkle, the political director for the

6 Illinois Federation of Teachers, and fellow union lobbyist

7 David Piccioli were the only people who took advantage

8 of a small window opened by law makers a few months earlier.

9 The legislation enabled union officials to get into the

10 state teachers' pension fund and <u>count</u> their previous years

11 as union employees after quickly obtaining teaching certificates and working

12 in a classroom. They just <u>had</u> to do it before the legislation was signed into

13 law.

14 Although the bill received bi-partisan support, the

15 benefit to union officials <u>was sponsored</u> by Springfield Democrats showered

16 by IFT campaign contributions during the 2006 campaigns. 15

142 words

Example A. Getting from Unedited to Edited

Line 1 unedited

> Two lobbyists...<u>were allowed</u> **(passive voice)** *change* **to:**

Line 1 edited

> One day of substitute teaching <u>qualified</u> **(action verb, active voice)** *two lobbyists*

Line 3-4 unedited

> **Change** <u>has found</u> to <u>found</u> (nearly the same meaning, one less word) (See FAQs p. 59 on difference between simple past tense and present perfect tense)

Line 7 unedited

> **Change** Preckwinkle...and David Piccioli <u>were</u> **("to be" verb)**

Line 6 edited

> **to:** Preckwinkle...Piccioli <u>gained access</u> to **(action verb)** Line

7-13 unedited

> **Shorten**...were the only people who took advantage of a small window opened by lawmakers a few months earlier. The legislations enabled union officials to get into the state teachers pension fund and count their previous years as union employees after quickly obtaining teaching certificates and working in a classroom **to:**

Line 6-9 edited

> <u>gained access</u> **(action verb)** to the teachers' pension fund by obtaining teaching certificates and teaching in a classroom for a single day before the bill <u>became</u> law. The law then <u>allowed</u> **(action verb)** them to count their years spent as union employees as teaching years.

Line 15-18 unedited

> **Clarify:** Although the bill received bi-partisan support, the benefit to union officials <u>was sponsored</u> **(passive voice)** by Springfield Democrats showered by IFT campaign contributions during the 2006 campaign

to:

Line 10-13 – edited

> The two <u>had taken</u> **(action verb)** advantage of a little-known provision (edited) of a 2007 pension fund bill which passed with bi-partisan support in Springfield. Senate Democrats, showered with IFT campaign contributions during the 2006 elections, <u>had sponsored</u> **(action verb)** the benefit to union officials.

Example A. (edited)

Sub for a Day, Teacher Pension for Life

1   One day of substitute teaching in 2007 <u>qualified</u> two lobbyists, with

2   no prior teaching experience, to participate legally in the State of Illinois'

3   teachers pension fund.

4   A Tribune WGN-TV Investigation <u>found</u> that Steven Preckwinkle,

5   political director for the Illinois Federation of Teachers, and fellow union

6   lobbyist David Piccioli <u>gained</u> access to the teachers pension fund by obtaining

7   teaching certificates and teaching in a classroom for a single day before the bill

8   <u>became</u> law. The law then <u>allowed</u> them to count their years spent as union

9   employees as teaching years.

10   The two <u>had taken</u> advantage of the little-known provision of a 2007

11   pension fund bill that had passed with bi-partisan support in Springfield.

12   Senate Democrats, showered with IFT campaign contributions

13   during the 2006 elections, <u>had sponsored</u> the benefit to union officials.

130 words

EXAMPLE B. (unedited)

1   If openness means to "go with the flow," it is necessarily an

2   accommodation to the present. That present is so closed to doubt

3   about so many things impeding the progress of its principles that

4   unqualified openness to it would mean forgetting the despised

5   alternative to it, knowledge of which makes us aware of what is

6   doubtful in it.[16]

     63 words

EXAMPLE B. (edited)

1   If an open mind means to "go with the flow," it follows that we accept

2   the present and its absolute certainty about its principles. Going with the

3   flow also means we ignore any alternatives to those principles,

4   crucial knowledge that would warn us of whatever is doubtful in

5   them.

     54 words

a press release that gets picked up

Via email, a press release delivers news about a company (or organization) to the public that the company wants media and the wider world to know. It answers six questions about the news the company is releasing: **who, what, why, where, when** and **how.**[17]

Types of Press Releases:

A business announcement: If the company is public (sells its stock to outside investors), its press releases will include quarterly earnings reports, the introduction of new products or their recall, annual meetings and noteworthy employee hiring and promotions.

A death announcement or obituary is a special form of press release that usually informs the media of the death of a prominent person. The same questions apply: **who, what, how, when, where** and **why.**

Overall Form of a Press Release or Obituary

On company letterhead, double spaced.

One page if possible. Editors receive hundreds of press releases a week. A short, well-written release with a provocative headline and the answers to as many of the questions—who, what, how, when, where and why—packed into the lead paragraph have the best chance of escaping the trash.

Obituaries, however, are often longer than one page, determined by what the deceased has accomplished in life. Write in the active voice, in the third person. (He, she, they, them.)

Quote from a relevant employee/expert of the company that develops the key point(s) of the release. For an obituary, include quotes from colleagues, friends or relatives of the deceased.

Contact name, phone and email in upper-left hand corner;

Release Date and the words—FOR IMMEDIATE RELEASE—(ALL CAPS) in upper-right hand corner.

TITLE (centered) ALL CAPS, aka **HEADLINE**

A **subtitle** beneath the title suggests a news "hook" an editor can use. Upper and lower case.

Three number symbols centered at the bottom of the page signal the end of the press release.

###

COMPUTER COMMANDS to remember:

> **SELECT action verbs** instead of "**to be**" verbs.
>
> **BOLD** verbs and **BOLD** nouns **ESCAPE** the mundane.
>
> **DELETE** the dull, weak, diminishing words.
>
> **INSERT** the active voice for the passive voice.

Two sample press releases follow.

EXAMPLE A (hypothetical press release)

contact name	Date (the news should appear)
email and phone	FOR IMMEDIATE RELEASE

RIVAL BIG PHARMAS PEN "GREEN" AGREEMENT
Merck, Pfizer To Share Shipping Hub, Lessen Carbon Footprint

Pfizer and Merck, the country's two leading pharmaceutical manufacturers, today announced they will share warehouse and distribution facilities in an effort to lessen both companies' carbon footprint.

Total combined carbon emissions per year are expected to drop by 500,000 tons as a result of the companies' actions.

Talks between the two began after the President asked U.S. manufacturers to explore ways they can consolidate facilities in order to conserve energy and reduce carbon emissions.

Donald Dracus, environmental manager of Merck, contacted his opposite number at Pfizer, Martin Malloy, and the two worked out ways to share their refrigerated storage and shipping facilities in New York, Maine, Ohio, Kansas and Florida. Key issues resolved were confidential shipping statistics and product storage safety.

Jeffrey Kindler, CEO of Pfizer and Richard T. Clark, CEO of Merck, issued a joint statement praising the consolidation, saying: "This is cooperation every sector of U.S. business needs to pursue if we're going to combat global warming in a meaningful way."

###

Example B (obituary)

contact name   Date (the news should appear)

email and phone   FOR IMMEDIATE RELEASE

IRA 'YAR' YARBROUGH
Cartoonist drew "Superman"

Ira "Yar" Yarbrough, a former Rogers Park cartoonist, drew the "Superman" comic strip in the 1940s, and later had his own nationally syndicated strip, "Tallulah," which ran in 200 newspapers.

A memorial mass will be said for Mr. Yarbrough, 72, at 11:00 a.m. March 26, 1983, at the Episcopal Church of the Advent, 2900 Logan Blvd. in Chicago. Mr. Yarbrough had retired in 1976 to Englewood, Florida, and died February 28 in an Arcadia, FL hospital from complications of Alzheimer's disease.

"My father loved cartooning," his daughter, Joan Kufrin, said.

"Our childhood was wonderful. He drew at home and we got to see what was going to happen before the other kids did. He ghosted 'Superman' for four years, during which he created the cartoon character of Mr. Mxyzptlk, a mischievous little guy from the fifth dimension. The only way Superman could get rid of him was to trick him into pronouncing his name backward."

Mr. Yarbrough started his own film animation firm, YAR/Animation, in Chicago, in 1958. Earlier, he had been an art director for Rand McNally & Co. and a cartographer and artist for the Missouri State Planning Board.

Survivors, besides his daughter, include his wife Harriet (Thesen), a son, Ira Jr., and six grandchildren.

###

PRACTICE

Using examples as reference, **write** a press release based on recent news of your company or organization.

Write an obituary of an acquaintance who has died.

Read the next chapter. Choose a company or organization you'd like to research further in order to write a marketing plan for them, based on a product they make or a service they offer.

Review the 20 nouns for "asset."

write a marketing plan

Companies constantly search for new business and new clients. A marketing plan proposes a way for the company to sell its product(s) to a new group of consumers and shows how that will affect the bottom line.[18] A thorough, well-written marketing plan answers the questions **what, why, who, when, where** and **how.** The following is an outline of the typical marketing plan.

1. Introduction:

    State the company's mission statement. If there is none, draft one to keep you on track as you write the marketing plan.

    > A mission statement tells what a company does and how, and explains its ideals and main purpose.

2. Subject: A New Market for ABCORP   **what**

3. The goal   **why**
    An overview of the market research that identifies and targets a new, potential market or a niche (specialty) market, and how it ties into the corporate mission.

4. The environment or situation of your company   **who/what**
    - Detail the services/products your company currently provides
    - Describe your customers—who, how many, why they buy your product
    - Describe existing segments of the market and your company's percentage of sales
    - Identify opportunity for growth: the new market and projected sales
    - State overall strengths and weaknesses of your company

5. The environment or situation of the competition   **who/what**
    - Detail the services/products the competition currently provides.
    - Describe competition's customers—who, how many, why they buy competing products
    - Describe existing segments of the market and percentages of sales of each
    - State overall strengths and weaknesses of competition

6.   The Big Picture, or Beyond the Marketplace   **what**

          Include factors that can act either as opportunities
          (or threats) to the plan:

- Technology
- Economy
- Politics
- Culture, society

7.   The Marketing Strategy   **what**

        Product Introduction

- New name?
- Special pricing?
- Unusual guarantee?
- New packaging?
- New, upgraded features?
- Time-sensitive offer?

        Promotion   **how/when**

- Advertising
- Public relations
- Social media
- Direct marketing
- Special promotions

        Distribution   **where**

- Offer better margins to distributors?
- Exclusive distributorship for limited time?
- New locations for product?

        Pricing Strategy   **what**

        The factors that may affect price:

- List price vs. discounts
- Payment terms
- Financing
- Leasing

8.   Servicing the New Market   **how**

9.   Achievable Goals   **what**

10.   Monitoring Results   **how**

11.   The Bottom Line including: **what**
             Additional personnel needed
             Test marketing
             Legal requirements
             Profit potential
             Total costs of the plan

12.   Summary and recommendations (if asked for by management)

PRACTICE:

Using the outline, **research** and **write** a marketing plan for a product, made by the company you've chosen, to introduce it into new markets. If it is a real product, use actual data to make the case for or against the outcome.

Read the next chapter. Be thinking of a new project or undertaking that your chosen company can be considering: new quarters; new location; new computer technology; and how a feasibility study can help the company decide what to do.

Add 15 synonyms for the noun "idea" to your life list. Yes, there are.

tcpneco	nporiptcee	soehshpyti
heecsm	tjeebvioc	lparsopo
ima	lago	ththuog
npooiin	kgniinl	nsiopmires
alpn	nitnioent	toonin

write a feasibility study

A feasibility study explores the wisdom of a company/organization's plan to pursue a new opportunity or undertaking: going into a new business; extending existing business into a new territory; new construction; new technology. A well-researched and well-written feasibility study is especially critical when making "Go/No Go" decisions regarding entry into new ventures.[19]

THINK ABOUT

Before writing a word, what is the first step? Read the company's mission statement. Make sure every factor in the study is compatible with the mission. If a company does not have a mission statement, consider drafting a sample, based on what you already know about the company.

Based on your reading of this chapter, what are the key questions to be answered in a feasibility study? And which is the most important? In this instance: **what** and **why** are key; **who, how, when** and **where** follow logically.

INTRODUCE the elements of a typical feasibility study, each answering specific questions.

a. State the project proposal, usually as a question.
    Should ABCORP Build New Headquarters?   **what**

b. Background for the proposal—**what** the current situation is.

c. Reason(s) for proposed change   **why**

d. Costs and benefits (pros and cons) affecting proposal: **what**
    Economics
    Technology and systems
    Operations
    Legal concerns
    Culture
    Environment

e. Those affected by the new venture   **who/how**

f. Requirements and costs
    Staff   **who**
    Equipment   **what**
    Real estate   **where**

g.	Proposed timetable	**when**
h.	X Factors (variables that can affect the outcome of the operation that may not yet have been considered.)	**what**

> Real estate market forces
> Economy
> Scheduling
> Geography
> Impact on customers

i.	Final recommendation for or against proceeding with the project.	**why**

Which **COMPUTER COMMANDS** are most relevant to a feasibility study?

BOLD verbs and nouns;
CENTER your key idea(s);
SELECT action verbs instead of "to be" verbs.
INSERT the active voice for the passive voice wherever you find it.
ESCAPE the mundane.
SHIFT not your point of view.
DELETE the extraneous.
QUIT on a thoughtful note.

Key takeaway: All company studies or plans need to be compatible with the company's mission.

Key takeaway: Structure any feasibility study or plan to ask—and answer—the questions: what, why, who, how, when and where.

PRACTICE:

Using the above outline for your feasibility study and actual research data, **make the case for** or **against** your project.

FAQs about grammar,
usage and meanings of words

Q.   What is the difference in usage between **anybody** and **any body?**

A.   Use **anybody** when you mean any person. Use **any body** when you mean any corpse, any human organization, or any group. The same rule applies to nobody, somebody, or everybody.

Q.   Which is correct?
    1.   The material in this class worries **you and I.**
    2.   The material in this class stays **between you and me.**

A.   Never substitute "I" as the object of a preposition or verb. **Hint:** You would not say "The material in this class worries I." When in doubt, say the preposition or verb with "I" and without "you" and you'll know which is correct.

Q.   What is the difference between "**can** I?" and "**may** I?"

A.   No matter how interchangeable they are when used in informal conversation ("Can I just cut in line here?"), when writing, remember "can" and "may" are not interchangeable. "Can" means the ability or power to do something. "May" asks permission to do it.[20]

Q.   What does it mean to **conjugate** a verb?

A.   It simply means to make a systematic list of all the various forms of a verb, based on who is doing the action. In English, most verbs change form only slightly no matter who is doing the action. I laugh. You laugh. He laughs. She laughs. We laugh. You (all) laugh. They laugh.

      However, one verb in English does change depending on who is doing the action. That is the verb "to be," the one most often conjugated.

The verb **"to be"**

Present/singular	**Present/plural**	**Past/singular**	**Past/plural**
I am	we are	I was	we were
you are	you are	you were	you were
he, she, it is	they are	he, she, it was	they were

Future/singular	**Future/plural**	**Present perfect sing.**	**Present Perf.Plural**
I will be	we will be	I have been	we have been
you will be	you will be	you have been	you have been
he, she, it will be	they will be	he, she, it has been	they have been

Past perfect sing.	**Past perfect pl.**	**Future perfect sing.**	**Fut. Perf. plural**
I had been	We had been	I will have been	We will have been
You had been	You had been	You will have been	You will have been
He, she, it had been	They had been	He, she it will have been	They will have been

Q.   What is a **gerund,** *aka a verbal?*

A.   It is the *–ing* form of the verb when it is used as a noun, as in "Laughing is good for the soul."

Q.   What is a **hypothesis?**

A.   (1) a tentative explanation for an observation, phenomenon, or scientific problem that can be tested by further investigation;

(2) something taken to be true for the purpose of argument or investigation;

(3) an assumption.

Q.   What is an **infinitive?**

A.   The form of a verb that does not change to indicate a particular tense or number or person, used with or without the word "to."
ex: "Let them laugh." "It doesn't hurt to laugh." "We want to walk."

Q.   **Lie** and **lay.** Which is correct?

She is laying down now. She is lying down now.

A.   She is lying down.

Lie is an intransitive verb. An intransitive verb (such as lie or die,) does not take an object.[21]

Its parts include:

Present tense:	lie	I lie in bed.
Past tense:	lay	I lay there for hours.
Present participle:	is lying	I'm lying down now.
Past participle:	lain	I have lain there many times.

Lay is a transitive verb, meaning its action takes an object.
Its parts include:

Present tense:	lay	I lay the book on the table.
Past tense:	laid	I laid the book there earlier.
Present participle	is laying	He is laying his cards on the table.
Past participle	has laid	She has laid her clothes out for the day.

Q.   What is a **past participle?**

A.   It is formed by adding "ed" to the base form of a verb to describe a completed action or past condition. He was discouraged. She has just arrived.[22]

Q. What is a **preposition?**

A. It is a *linking* word: *in, on, beyond, behind, by, to, since, from, over, across, down, of, off,* etc., used to show a noun's relationship to another noun, word or phrase in a sentence.

> **ex:** Let's put our cards **on** the table. (The preposition **on** shows the relationship between cards and table.)

> **ex:** This marketing report goes **beyond** my expectations. (The preposition **beyond** links expectations with the marketing report.)

Q. What is a **present participle,** (also a verbal)?

A. It is the *–ing* form of the verb when it's used as an adjective as in "Years ago, dentists administered laughing gas to patients for pain." Or, it is *ing* added to the base form of the verb in continuing and/or progressive verb forms like go*ing*, leav*ing*, dy*ing*.

Q. What is a **pronoun?**

A. A small class of short words (*I, you, it, he, she, we, they, this, who, what, everyone, someone,* etc.) used to replace a noun(s), or other pronoun(s). Pronouns keep you from repeating that noun, thus keeping sentences short.

> **ex:** Tell the marketing team **they** can use the conference room tomorrow.

> instead of

> Tell the marketing team that the marketing team can use the conference room tomorrow.

> **ex:** Is **everyone** here aboard with the plan?

> instead of

> Are all the employees in this room aboard with the plan?

Q. What is a **tense?**

A. It is the form of a verb that shows *when* something happens. For example:

Tense	Example
Present	I laugh.
Past	I laughed.
Future	I will laugh.
Present perfect	I have laughed.
Past perfect	I had laughed.
Future perfect	I will have laughed.

Present progressive	I am laughing.
Past progressive	I was laughing.
Future progressive	I will be laughing.
Present perfect progressive	I have been laughing.
Past perfect progressive	I had been laughing.
Future perfect progressive	I will have been laughing.

Which tenses are easier to understand? Which tenses contribute to concise and precise writing?

Q. How do you use **who** or **whom** correctly?

A. It depends on how the word is used in the sentence. If the word is the object of a preposition, use whom:

> **ex:** For **whom** does the bell toll? (object of preposition **for**)
>
> **ex:** To **whom** shall I address this letter? (object of preposition **to**)

When the word is the subject of a verb, or a clause, use **who.**

> **ex:** **Who** (shall I say) is calling? (**Who** is the subject of **is calling.**)
>
> **ex:** Students **who** don't do homework are not interested in succeeding.
>
> (**Who** is the subject of the clause **"don't do homework."**)

Here is a shortcut to help you decide. Substitute **she** or **he** for the **who** in a sentence, and **her** or **him** for the **whom** in a sentence you're unsure of, and you'll be able to quickly tell which is correct.

In other words: she or he = who

   her or him = whom

ex: **To who/whom** was the letter addressed?

The letter was addressed to she/her.

If she = who, and her = whom, it's clear the answer is whom.

ex: **Who/whom** shall I say is calling?

Shall I say he/ him is calling?

If he = who and him = whom, it's clear the answer is who. [23]

index

A

B

C

D

E

F

G

H

I

K

L

M

endnotes

[1] Tenney, Edward A., and Wardle, Ralph M., *A Primer for Readers*. (New York: F.S. Croft and Co., 1943), p. 36.

[2] Using English.com. http://www.usingenglish.com/glossary/adverb.html accessed May 19, 2010).

[3] Strunk, William. *Elements of Style*. Ithaca, N.Y.: Priv. print. [Geneva, N.Y.: Press of W.P. Humphrey], 1918; Write with Nouns and Verbs: *Elements of Style with revisions, an introduction and a new chapter on writing by E. B. White*. (New York: The Macmillan Company, 1959), p. 57-58; Bartleby.com, 1999. www.bartleby.com/141/

[4] Simmons, Robin L., 1997-2009. http://www.chompchomp.com/terms/completesentence.htm. (accessed June 30, 2009).

[5] The Modals. http://www.csulb.edu/colleges/cla/departments/english/wrl/handouts/modal-verbs (accessed April 13, 2009).

[6] Improve Your English BY YOURSELF. Hi2En.com.2009-2010. http://hi2en.com/grammar.aspx?Id=73 (accessed April 13, 2009).

[7] It is so easy that The Radicati Group , which tracks these phenomena, reports that in 2019, more than 293 billion business and consumer emails will be sent and received *each day*. *Worldwide*.

[8] https://www.radicati.com/wp/wp-content/uploads/2018/12/Email-Statistics-Report-2019-2023- Executive-Summary.pdf

[9] Stavins, Richard, attorney at law, Robbins, Salomon & Patt, Ltd., Chicago, IL., June, 2012.

[10] Heathfield, Susan M., updated February 04, 2019. https://www.thebalancecareers.com/internet-and-email-policy-sample-1918869

[11] Davis, Kenneth, W., Ph.D., *Business Writing and Communication,* second edition, (McGraw-Hill, 2010),

p. 51.

[12] Abell, Alicia, *Business Style, Grammar and Usage. Boston, MA:* (Aspatore Books, 2003), p. 114.

[13] Strunk, William. *Elements of Style*. Ithaca, N.Y.: Priv. print. [Geneva, N.Y.: Press of W.P. Humphrey], 1918.

"Be Clear." *Elements of Style with revisions, an introduction and a new chapter on writing by E. B. White*. (New York; Macmillan Company. 1959), p. 65 ; Bartleby.com, 1999. www.bartleby.com/141/

[14] Strunk, William. *Elements of Style.* Ithaca, N.Y.: Priv. print. [Geneva, N.Y.: Press of W.P. Humphrey], 1918; "Avoid the Use of Qualifiers." *Elements of Style with revisions, an introduction and a new chapter on writing by E. B. White.* (New York: Macmillan Company. 1959), p. 59; Bartleby.com, 1999. www.bartleby.com/141/

[15] Long, Ray and Grotto, Jason, "Sub for a Day, Teacher Pension for Life," *Chicago Tribune,* October 22, 2011.

[16] Bloom, Allen, "The Closing of the American Mind," http://www.pc.maricopa.edu/ss/phi101/II/II_E_Introduction Our Virtue

[17] Stollar and Bard Communications. "What Is A Press Release?" 2009. http://www.publicityinsider.com/release.asp (accessed August 31, 2009).

[18] Business Resource Software, Inc. 1994-2009. http://www.businessplans.org/Market.html (accessed July 22, 2009).

[19] Writing a Feasibility Study. http://nfsmi.org/documentlibraryfiles/PDF/20080212032917.pdf (accessed November, 2009).

[20] Bernstein, Theodore M. *The Careful Writer.* *A Modern Guide to English Usage.* (New York: Atheneum, 1965, 1980), p. 87-88.

[21] Answers.com. Grammar Dictionary http://www.answers.com/topic/verb (accessed July 1, 2009).

[22] UsingEnglish.com—Term: Participle http://www.usingenglish.com/glossary/participles.html (accessed June 24, 2010).

[23] Straus, Jane. *The Blue Book of Grammar and Punctuation.* (California: Jossey-Bass, 2006 http://www.grammarbook.com/whoVwhom.asp (accessed July 14, 2010).

What business writers are saying about WriteTight, EditTough®

WriteTight, EditTough® is a beacon for lost writers adrift in a sea of words…a small masterpiece. I learned more than I ever did in English class.
Allan Cox
author of ten best-selling business books
Your Inner CEO is the most recent.

In the corporate world, Joan Kufrin has a proven track record of writing tight and editing tough, and of coaching others to do the same. Now Joan has created a road map for others to achieve this same goal, consistently, concisely, and across all types of business writing. Do yourself a favor. Read this book and keep it handy while you write.
Lael Lyons
consultant, training and information design
co-author of *"Yes, But…The Top 40 Killer Phrases and How You Can Fight Them"*

WriteTight, EditTough® is essential for business people who expect results from their writing. This practical, easy-to-use book will ramp up your writing skills so every message you deliver packs a "winning" punch. Whether you're new to business writing or more seasoned, you'll find this book extremely helpful. It's a must-read.
Susan Shahoda
director, HR Communications, UCLA

I have always been awed by Joan Kufrin's ability to put intricate thoughts into compelling words or to create an outstanding manuscript—whatever the subject. Write Tight, Edit Tough® eloquently and concisely provides the business person with the best of her business skills.
Ella D. Strubel
executive vice president, (ret.) Leo Burnett Worldwide

I have edited and proofed colleagues' articles for 45 years and often yearned for a simple book I could hand writers before they wrote a word to show them how to achieve copy that goes straight to the point. WriteTight, EditTough® is that book.
Rebecca Dixon
associate provost, (ret.) Northwestern University

Write Tight, Edit Tough® is an idea useful to any professional, whatever their field of endeavor and a wonderful reference for those who do writing as part of their professional life. The material gets right to the point without wasting words: the point of the course. I rediscovered some of what I had learned as a youth and have since forgotten, but was also introduced to new material—such as modals—which I had never been exposed to. It is good work.
Kurt O. Thomsen, Ph.D., PG
environmental consultant, KOT Environmental Consulting, Inc.

www.ingramcontent.com/pod-product-compliance
Lightning Source LLC
Chambersburg PA
CBHW081602170526
45166CB00009B/2795